"Zany humor.   lo-
lescents' questions about their changing bodies...soothing reassurances of the normalcy of
approaching puberty at different speeds...a sen-
sible and sensitive philosophy about growing up."
ALA Booklist

"Superlative...accurate concise information
about menses, puberty, and personal hy-
giene...Excellent for pre- and young teens...a
'must see.'"
Journal of Adolescent Health Care

"Funny and successful...presents much needed,
understandable and clear-cut information about
girls and puberty, and reinforces the idea of talking to adults and friends as an outlet for adolescent confusion...should be on everyone's best
film list."
Voice of Youth Advocates

"It's such a pleasure to see a film on an important
topic that is not only informative, but fun,
charming, delightful, and touching. DEAR
DIARY is a marvelous teaching tool and a won-
derful viewing experience!"
Dr. James Achtzehn,
School of Education and Human Services
Gallaudet College

Winner of numerous film awards, DEAR DIARY
focuses on the concerns of an adolescent girl as
she enters puberty. Using the same humor-
ous approach as its companion for boys, AM I
NORMAL?, DEAR DIARY covers the sensitive
issues of body development, breast size, menstruation, sexual feelings, masturbation, orgasm, and
peer pressure.

Other Avon Flare Books by
Jeanne Betancourt

AM I NORMAL?

Dear Diary

Jeanne Betancourt

Illustrations by
JEANNE BETANCOURT

Based on the film by
DEBRA FRANCO and DAVID SHEPARD

AN AVON FLARE BOOK

DEAR DIARY is an original publication of Avon Books.
This work has never before appeared in book form.

AVON BOOKS
A division of
The Hearst Corporation
959 Eighth Avenue
New York, New York 10019

Copyright © 1983 by Copperfield Films, Inc.
Published by arrangement with Copperfield Films, Inc.
Library of Congress Catalog Card Number: 82-16281
ISBN: 0-380-82057-9

Library of Congress Cataloging in Publication Data

Betancourt, Jeanne.
    Dear diary.

    (An Avon/Flare book)
    "Based on the film by Debra Franco and David
Shepard."
    Summary: Twelve-year-old Jane keeps a diary of
her secret thoughts and feelings about the changes
taking place in her mind and body.
    1. Sex instruction for girls.   2. Puberty—
Juvenile literature. [1. Sex instruction for girls.
2. Puberty]   I. Dear diary (Motion picture)
II. Title.
HQ51.B47 1983   613.9'55   82-16281
ISBN 0-380-82057-9

First Flare Printing, February, 1983

Thanks to Rosalie Williams, educational consultant to this book, for her expertise and support.

Special thanks to Lee Minoff, Charlotte Sheedy, Jean Feiwel and Sheldon Winicour for their invaluable assistance.

And, of course, all our love to Hillary, Shannon, and Carmele.

For my daughter

The photographs in this book are derived from the original motion picture, DEAR DIARY. The Director of Photography was Austin deBesche. Art Direction by Karla Clement.

CAST

JANIE	Hillary Ellin
MAUREEN	Shannon Dobson
CATHY	Carmele Wesley
MOM	Marilyn Duchin
MR. BAKER	Paul Dunn
BRA SALESLADY	Iola Lynn Hayes
COACH	Rose Weaver
ROGER	Jack Younger
ALSO APPEARING:	Barlow Adamson, Julie Arvedon, Rebecca Batal, Annie Burton, Mark Hassett, Laura Novelline, Mark Pitman, Nancy Pothier, Valerie Price, Eve Reis, Emily Stein, Michelle Williams, Alexandra Zaroulis

Private Property

of

Janie Miller

KEEP OUT
_____

(and that
means *you* !)

April 2

Dear Diary,

My Uncle Louie gave you to me on April Fools'
Day, which was my brother's tenth birthday. (It's
not a coincidence that my brother was born on April
Fools' Day.) My uncle gives me a present on my
brother's birthday so I won't feel left out. I say it's
a reward for putting up with my brother for another
year. The present is usually a joke, because it's April
Fools' Day.

"Janie," Uncle Louie said as I was unwrapping
you, "this is the most difficult book ever written."
As I flipped through all the blank pages, this little
card fell out.

April Fool!!!
Love,
Uncle Lou

Not one of his better jokes, but you, diary, are
one of his better presents. (Last year he gave me a
box of rubber chocolates.)

I think keeping a diary will be fun. I'm going to write in you every day and tell you my secret thoughts and feelings. I like the idea of having a place where I can say anything I want without worrying about someone else thinking I'm silly or telling other people.

This is a place for keeping secrets and letting off steam.

I'll start by describing myself.

My name is Jane, but most everybody calls me Janie. I'd rather be called Jane.

I'm twelve and a half years old and go to Central Junior High.

My friends say I'm "cute," which means I'm pretty in an ordinary kind of way.

If you look at my picture you'll see what I mean.

My hair is *kind of* shiny.

My eyes are *kind of* big.

My skin is *kind of* nice.

All in all, I figure I'm *kind of* pretty.

The only thing about me that isn't *kind of* is my figure. I don't have one.

That's one of the things that's been bugging me lately.

These are my two best friends.
That's Cathy.

She's *very* pretty and has a wonderful personality. She's the type who tries to keep everybody happy. She says that's because she's a Libra and Libras like to keep everything balanced and peaceful.

Cathy believes in astrology. I'm not so sure I do, but I love to listen to her talking about it.

When Cathy grows up she wants to be a dancer. Or maybe a veterinarian.

This is Maureen.

She's *very* into the way she looks. During our history final last year she did up her fingernails in shocking pink. (She says on big occasions a girl *must* look her best.)

Maureen's fun to be with, but she's also *very* bossy. Cathy says that's because she's a Capricorn.

When Maureen grows up, she wants to be gorgeous.

Me? My birthday's June seventeenth, which makes me a Gemini. Ambitious and sensitive—that's me!

I'm going to be a runner, or maybe a dentist when I grow up. I love to run, more than anything. I'm the fastest runner in our gym class. Now I'm working on endurance.

My dad says that if I keep it up, when I'm in high school he'll take me to run in the Boston Marathon.

By the way, Maureen runs too. After boys.

Cathy, Maureen, and I have been best buddies since third grade, when Miss Roberts put us together to do a mural on "Jobs in Our Town."

We've always liked the same things and felt the same about stuff like favorite teachers and what to do on Saturday afternoon, and what to have on a pizza.

But that's all changing fast.

Now all Maureen thinks about, talks about, even reads about, is boys, boys, boys. And it seems Cathy is getting the same way.

Me and boys? I like them all right, but I've got more pressing things on my mind right now. Like the fact that Maureen, Cathy, and I don't even look the same age anymore.

Maureen looks about sixteen.
Cathy looks about fourteen.
And I look about *ten!*
If you did silhouettes of the three of us sideways they would look something like this:

9

The girls in my class are all excited about being teen-agers. It's all they *care* about. It's all they *ever* talk about.

"Did you get your period?"

"When are you going to start wearing a bra?"

"Will your mother let you wear makeup?"

"How often do you wash your hair?"

"What kind of deodorant do you use?"

"Do you think Tommy Granger is cute?"

And wouldn't you know, I'm probably the only girl in our entire junior high who hasn't gotten her period. (Well, maybe not the *only* one, but it sure feels that way sometimes.)

So you see, diary, I have lots to talk about. Thanks for listening.

~~Janie~~ Jane

P.S. Don't tell a soul!

April 3
Dear Diary,

I finished my math and science homework, but before I do my social studies I'm going to keep my promise to write in you every day.

A good example of the sort of thing that's been bothering me lately happened after gym.

Maureen was reading from her teen beauty magazine.

That's where she gets all kinds of juicy advice, like how to make an avocado face mask and why it's good to rinse your hair with beer and ten ways to get *him* to notice you.

I was feeling really good about my three-mile run and calculating in my head how many seconds faster I was than last week, when Maureen announced some calculations of her own.

"Hey, girls, listen to this." She read from her latest issue of *Cosmopoliteen* magazine. "'The ideal measurements for a woman are thirty-six-inch bust, twenty-four-inch waist, and thirty-six-inch hips.'"

Now, like I told you, I'm straight as an arrow. No curves.

Twenty-five-inch bust.

Twenty-five-inch waist.

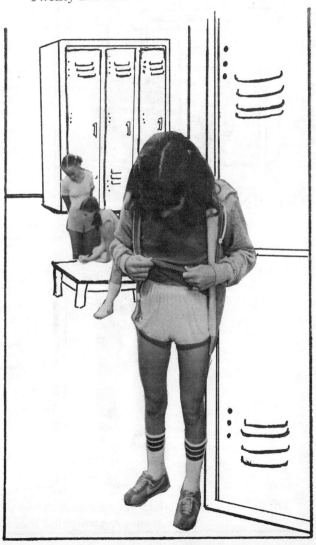

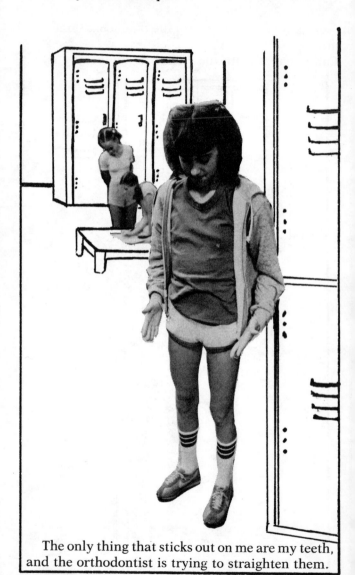

The only thing that sticks out on me are my teeth, and the orthodontist is trying to straighten them.

I decided she was getting carried away with all this perfect-body stuff, so I reminded her, "There are more important things in life than looks, Maureen."

Cathy agreed with me. "They do say beauty is only skin deep, Maureen."

But Maureen just batted her Shades of Night violet eyelids. "Yeah? Listen, when you watch TV, *who* gets the guy? *Who* wears the nice clothes? *Who* gets rich in the end?"

Cathy and I looked at one another and shrugged. "Who?"

"The pretty girl, that's who."

The pretty girl? Does she really believe looks are everything?

That's ridiculous. But when I think of the TV shows and commercials I watch, I half believe her. Then I half don't. I was about to *try* to explain how TV isn't the same as real life when the bell rang for our next class and we had to start rushing.

Good old Keep-the-Peace Cathy sighed, "Maybe you're right, Maureen." She checked herself out in the locker mirror. "Quick, Maureen, let me borrow your eye shadow."

When I look in the locker mirror, the light reflects off my shiny braces so that all I see is *glare*.

Terrific.

Jane

P.S. I do have the beginning of a bust, but no one can tell but me.

April 4
Dear Diary,

Today Maureen, Cathy, and I were hanging out in my room without anything in particular to do. I was feeling pretty depressed thinking over what Maureen said about having a perfect figure.

She must have guessed, because she put her arm around my shoulder and said, "Poor Janie. Twelve and a half and still a little girl. Look, cheer up, because I'm going to help you." She looked at Cathy. "We're going to teach Janie how to be a *woman*."

Cathy and I just looked at her. "How?" we asked.

"Let's see." Maureen thought for a few seconds. Then she snapped her fingers. "I got it. We'll start with a basic skill every girl *must* have—how to kiss a boy."

The truth about me and kissing boys is this: I've only done it twice, when we played Spin the Bottle at Maureen's boy-girl parties. Kissing boys is embarrassing enough, but in public! I managed not to play for too long. At the first party I offered to get more sodas from the kitchen and at the second one I stood guard. No one minded because there were more girls than boys at the parties anyway.

I decided this lesson couldn't hurt me and might be fun.

"Before we begin," Cathy suggested, "let's get the right mood."

"Perfect," Maureen answered. "Close the blinds and light some of that orange-blossom incense. Janie, go get your dad's cologne."

After she splashed Old Spice all over my smile pillow, she got very businesslike. "All right. Let's begin. These are Maureen's Five Steps to a Great Kiss.

"Step One: *Choose the right moment.*

"This is a boy, okay?" She held up my smile pillow. "You're sitting at the movies. You wait until the romantic part, when everything's all kissy-kissy, you know. That's what I mean by a 'right moment.'"

"Step Two: *Get closer.*

"You sort of lean into him, like this." She snuggled up to my pillow. "And he'll kind of stretch out and put his arm around your shoulder."

Cathy added, "You'll feel his hand begin to sweat." (I guess she's had more experience at kissing boys than I have.)

"Which means," Maureen concluded, "that he likes you."

"Step Three: *Flutter your eyelids for exactly three seconds.*

"Come on, try it."

I figured you have to learn sometime, so I fluttered, one—two—three.

"Good," Maureen said. "Just a little faster and you've got it.

"Step Four: *On the last flutter, pucker up.*" She squinched her lips together in a pucker. "Now," she said, "you try."

I took a deep breath of orange-blossom incense and followed Maureen's instructions, "Lean forward, flutter one, flutter two, flutter three, pucker."

Cathy was laughing. We were having fun, like when we used to take different parts in our favorite TV shows and act them out.

"Great," said Maureen. "You're ready for Step Five: *Kiss him*. First watch." Maureen got this faraway romantic look as she gazed into the eyes of my smile pillow, batted her eyelids one—two—three, puckered up, and kissed it for a real long time. She seemed to be getting very wiggly and emotional.

After what seemed like forever she ended the kiss and handed me the pillow. "Your turn."

I hesitated. I didn't want to get all emotional the way Maureen did.

"It's easy," she said. "Go ahead."

I held the pillow close and started fluttering my eyelids.

Cathy interrupted, "Tell Janie how it feels, Maureen."

"Oh, yeah, you feel mushy all over. Even *down there*."

I thought about the times I've felt mushy "down there." Like when I see a movie with some sexy scenes in it, or while I read my mom's romantic novel with lots of sappy love scenes, or even sometimes when I just *think* about kissing a boy.

Why does it happen, dear diary, and what does it mean?

I almost asked Maureen and Cathy, but it was embarrassing enough to kiss a pillow.

I want to know what's going on—and not going on—in my body, especially "down there."

Good night, dear diary,

Jane

P.S. I still don't know how to kiss a boy, but I had a great time with my friends.

P.P.S. Today I ran three miles in thirty minutes. That's my fastest yet.

April 7
Dear Diary,

I haven't written in a couple of days, because we had a track meet and I was real busy with that and my homework.

We won. Yay! Coach Anderson says if I keep it up I'm sure to make first-string next year.

That makes you think my problems are over, doesn't it? Well, wait until you hear what happened after school today.

Cathy and Maureen met me at my locker, as usual, so we could hang out together, as usual.

Maureen put her arm around my shoulder. I knew she was up to something.

"Depends on what it is," I answered.

"Well, now that you know how to kiss, it's time for you to get a boyfriend," Maureen explained.

"Perfect," Cathy agreed. She turned to me, "Who do you like?"

Diary, there's something I haven't told even you. There's a guy, Roger, in the eighth grade, who's real cute and the *best* on our running team. Whenever I think about what it would be like to have a boyfriend, he's the guy I think of.

So I told Maureen and Cathy, "Well, there's this guy, Roger, who likes to run." (The words just popped out before I could stop myself. Sometimes I'm really *dumb!*)

Cathy knew just who I meant. "Oooh, he's cute."

Maureen loved it. "Perfect, put your sneakers back on. Let's go."

Maureen dragged us down to the track, hatching a plan as she went.

Roger was there, all right, just like every after-noon, running round and round on the quarter-mile track.

Maureen reviewed the scheme one more time. Cathy double-checked it with me. "Now, do you know what to do?"

While I did my warm-up stretches I recited, "I run toward him. When I'm three paces from him, I wave."

"And don't forget to give him a big smile so he'll be sure to notice you," Maureen interrupted.

"Right," I continued. "Then he'll turn and run alongside me."

"Perfect!" Maureen positively glowed. "It'll be the beginning of a great romance."

I figured it this way. Running together would be a little bit like a date, except I wouldn't have to worry about talking and kissing.

For one foolish moment I even thought Maureen might have a good idea after all.

I ran onto the track. It felt great to be running. As I turned the first bend I could see Roger running toward me.

He moved so beautifully. I adjusted my stride to match the rhythm of his.

Has he noticed me yet? I wondered.

I felt free and easy. The breeze rushed by me.

I was floating toward him and he was floating toward me.

Just like in the movies.

Destiny.

We were about to meet.

I smiled.

As we passed one another I thought, *Just about now he should turn around and run next to me.*

I turned my head to greet him...

...and tripped.

I fell flat on my face in the dirt. Terrific! A runner who falls over her own feet trying to get a guy's attention.

Roger kept on running without even turning around.

It was a soft landing, so maybe he didn't hear me fall. Maybe he didn't even see me in the first place, which is what I hope.

Just like in the movies, all right—a disaster movie!

I made Cathy and Maureen take a "cross-your-heart-and-hope-to-die" oath that they will never ever say anything to anyone about me and Roger—or about what happened today. I'd die if he knew how much I like him.

I think I'll concentrate on running—alone!

Gotta go. Mom's calling me for supper.

Jane

P.S. I really blew it today, diary. Do you think I'll ever grow up?

April 8, 7:00 P.M.
Dear Diary,

Remember I was going to supper when I signed off? Well, during supper I was still thinking about how silly I felt when I "fell for Roger" and not paying much attention to whatever my parents and dumb brother were talking about. I also wasn't very hungry and was sort of poking at my fruit salad when I noticed a sticky feeling in my underpants.

I excused myself and ran upstairs to the bathroom. I unzipped my jeans and pulled down my pants as fast as possible and there was *blood*. Not a lot like I expected—just a small dark-red stain. But no doubt about it—I've got my period. Isn't that terrific?

I took one of my mom's sanitary napkins from the hall closet and stuck it to a clean pair of underpants. Then I put on my tightest jeans and looked at myself every which way in the mirror—just to be sure no one can see any bulges or wrinkles from the pad. It feels a little strange having something in my pants like that, but I guess I'll get used to it.

I don't really feel much different, just a little achey in my stomach, like my legs feel sometimes after a long run.

Now that I've got it, I'm not so sure I like the idea of blood coming out of me like that. Is it possible to be happy and unhappy about something at the same time?

On the one hand, life might be easier now that I'm finally catching up with my friends. On the other hand, I have all these questions:

How long will it last?

Will I get it again next month or skip months the way Cathy does?

Where does the blood come from?

Why did it start *now* and not next month or last year?

Will I get cramps like my cousin Andrea?

And what about running? Can I go to gym? What if there's a big meet when I have my period? Will it slow me down?

I wish you could answer all my questions, dear diary. Since you can't, I guess I'll ask my mom. Mothers are supposed to know these things.

Jane

P.S. I'm so happy I finally got IT!

8:00 P.M.
Dear Diary,
   Back again. Here's what happened with my mom.
When I went downstairs she was right where I knew
she'd be—in the living room listening to the dish-
washer.

Ever since we got a dishwasher last year, after supper my mom listens to it while she has her tea. She says that way she can really appreciate how much work the dishwasher is doing for her.

Sometimes we listen together. That's when I can count on having my mom to myself. My dad's in the den watching the news on TV and my stupid brother is in his room thinking up new ways to be stupid.

Mom and I have had some nice talks while the dishwasher is on. We talk about stuff like my running, and what to do during summer vacation, and how her mother is feeling, and how good supper was. Tonight Mom was sitting on the edge of the couch stirring her tea when I came in.

I was excited but a little nervous. "Hi, Mom. Guess what?"

She looked up and smiled. "What, dear?"

I sat down on the couch next to her. "I got my period," I whispered in her ear.

"Oh, *Janie.*" She put her cup down and smiled. "How wonderful." She gave me a big hug and kiss. "My little girl's a woman now. It seems like just yesterday you were a tiny baby cuddled in my arms, and now you're a *woman.*"

My mother can be pretty mushy. She's the emotional type. But she can be practical, too, like right then she asked me, "Do you know where I keep the sanitary napkins?"

"Yes," I told her, "I took some."

"Good," she said, like that was all there was to discuss.

"But Mom, I have some questions. I mean, I'm not quite sure why it happens and stuff."

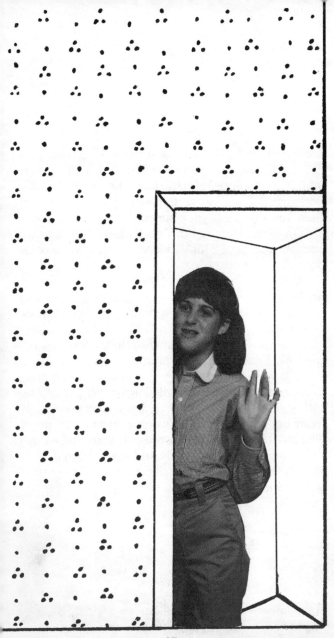

She sat up real straight and started fidgeting with her gold chain, the way she does when she's nervous. "Well, Janie," she started, "it happens so your body can have a baby. And when you're pregnant, then you don't get your period."

"Oh, I see," I said, but I really didn't. So I asked another question. "But why does blood have to come out?"

"Um—well, dear...you see..." She thought for a minute. "It's hard to explain. Let me think about it and see if I can't find a way to answer your question later."

I tried another one of my questions. "Can you tell me how long it will last, Mom?"

"Of course, dear, three to seven days. Everyone's cycle is different." She smiled again. "It's really exciting, isn't it? And honey, don't worry about it. Your body knows what it's doing, even if you don't. The most important thing is this is your body's way of telling you you're ready to have a baby." Then she added, real fast: "But of course you won't until you're married."

Babies? Marriage? That's the last thing on my mind!

Well, diary, Mom tried her best. I didn't want to tell her I'm more confused than ever.

I wonder if I should go to gym tomorrow? Will running make me bleed more? I better figure a way to bring sanitary napkins to school, so I can change them during the day.

This may be more trouble than it's worth.

Good night, diary.

Jane

P.S. I hope Mom knows enough to start buying twice as many sanitary napkins, because *I'm* sure not going to do it.

P.P.S. You must know how important you are to me since I wrote you three times in one day. I think I'll take you to school tomorrow.

April 9
Dear Diary,

Today was the first day of going to school with my period, and you won't *believe* what happened.

It was during science, which comes just before gym. Mr. Baker, our science teacher, is the cutest teacher we have this year. Maureen has a crush on him, which is why she sits in the center seat of the front row. I like him too. He's pretty neat, for a teacher.

I wasn't paying much attention to his class today because all I could think about was whether I should go to gym when I have my period.

So I sent a note to Maureen.

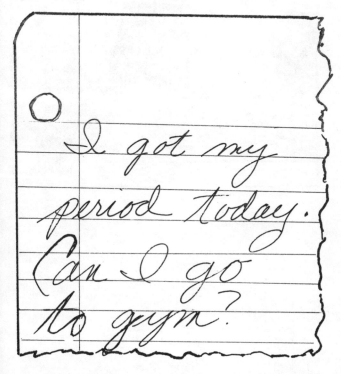

I folded it tight and stapled it so no one would read it but Maureen.

First, I handed it to Karen.

My eyes followed the note as Karen handed it to George.

George started to fool with the staple and turned around and grinned at me. I acted like I wasn't watching him, but I was real scared he'd open it.

Finally George handed it to Cathy.

Cathy handed it to Lillian, who handed it to Maureen.

I watched Maureen pull my note open.

Just then Mr. Baker stopped what he was doing. He eyed Maureen suspiciously.

"Is that a note, Maureen?" he asked as he walked toward her desk.

Maureen acted very offended, the way she does when she's been caught at something she's not supposed to be doing. "A note, Mr. Baker? I'd never..."

Before she could finish her phony excuse, Mr. Baker was back at his desk opening *my note.*

I thought I would die, right there in Room 390B. The whole class was perfectly quiet. Some kids turned and looked at me.

Mr. Baker has been known to read notes out loud, which is bad enough if it's a note like "Does Mike know you're in love with him?" or "Isn't Mr. Baker's tie ugly?"

But what if the note says "I got my period. Can I go to gym today?" And everybody knows who sent it?

I held my breath.

Mr. Baker looked around the room.

Please, Mr. Baker, I prayed. *Please don't read my note out loud.*

"Class," he began.

I covered my face with my hands.

Mr. Baker smiled and put my note in his pocket. "Class, how do you feel about...menstruation?"

Every girl in the class died. Not just me. And the boys acted like they were really disgusted. Dumb Larry Rivers even yelled out, "Oh, gross!"

Mr. Baker ignored our reactions and went over to the board and drew a diagram.

Right then and there he taught the whole class—boys and girls—about menstruation.

49

Menstruation is a normal and natural process that every woman goes through.

Every month a tiny egg leaves one of the two ovaries, and travels through a tube towards the uterus (or womb).

The travel of the egg is called OVULATION.

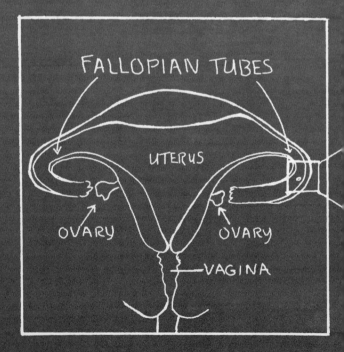

If the egg meets a male sperm while it is traveling, it is fertilized. If the fertilized egg reaches the uterus, it attaches to the wall of the uterus, and a pregnancy can begin.

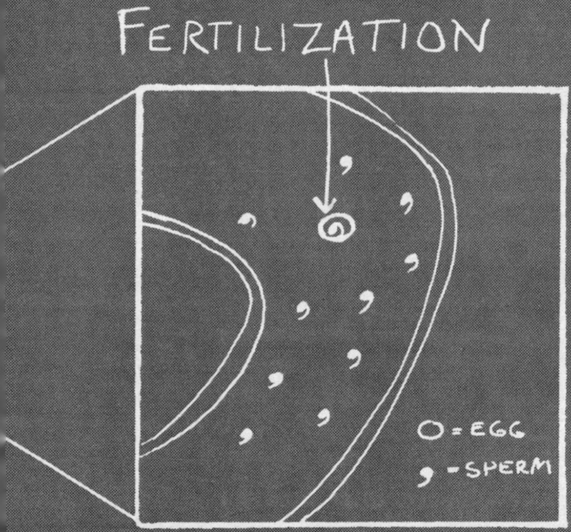

FERTILIZATION

O = EGG

ϑ = SPERM

At the same time, the uterus is getting ready for the egg. It builds up a lining of blood and tissue that would nourish and protect the fertilized egg as it grows into a baby.

Whether you are ready to have a baby or not, every month an egg will travel this same route.

If the egg is not fertilized—you will get your period. What is happening is that the lining formed by the uterus isn't needed—there is no fertilized egg to nourish and protect.

So the egg, and the lining, will simply flow out the vagina. That's the blood you see when you have your period.

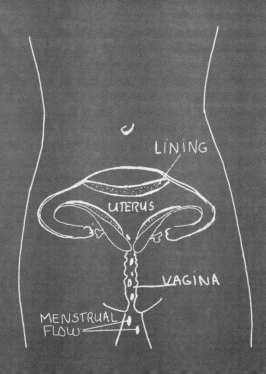

The process of shedding the egg and the lining out of the vagina is called MENSTRUATION. It will last for a few days, and then the cycle will begin again.

Two questions girls often ask are:

1. Will it happen every month?

2. How many days will it last?

The answer to both is—everybody's body is different. Many girls are not "regular." Especially during the first years of menstruation, you may miss months at a time. That's pretty normal.

As to how long it lasts—for one girl it could be one day, and for her best friend it could be seven days—or anywhere in between.

After Mr. Baker finished his explanation at the board, he moved back to his desk and brought up the baby business, just like my mom did.

"Now, this is important," he said. "When a girl begins to menstruate, it means she's capable of getting pregnant. But that *doesn't* mean she's ready to have a baby. For one thing, having a baby is a physically difficult experience, and your body won't really be ready to handle it until you're older.

"But just as important, you need to be *emotionally* ready, and that means being a grown-up—with a grown-up's responsibilities and maturity and experience in life."

Then, really casually, Mr. Baker said what he always says when he's finished explaining things.

"Any questions?"

Tommy Granger—the most popular guy in our class—raised his hand and asked a question! "Can girls do stuff? You know, like go to gym, go swimming, go horseback riding—things like that?"

I couldn't believe it. A guy asking a question about *this*. I was on the edge of my seat waiting to hear what Mr. Baker would say.

"Yes, it's perfectly all right. A girl can wear a tampon or pad and do anything she wants. She can do all kinds of exercise—skating, swimming, dancing, running. And no one will know she's having her period.

"The most important thing to remember is this—menstruation is a *healthy* and *normal* part of growing up for girls.

"Just think—at one time or another, over half the people in the world—menstruate!"

I felt much better about having my period when he said that.

I thought of a question, so I raised my hand.

The instant the words came out of my mouth I remembered I was in a class full of kids—half of them *boys*.

But then, Tommy Granger had asked a question and no one laughed. They didn't laugh at me either.

Mr. Baker answered in that same casual voice. "Well, some girls—and women—do get backache or mild cramps. Others may feel nothing at all. It usually goes away in a few hours. If anyone has severe pain, of course then she should see a doctor or nurse."

The bell rang. As we started to get up, Mr. Baker called out, "And if you have any more questions, come see me during home room. I'll be happy to talk to you."

As we were leaving, Maureen came over to me and whispered, "Congratulations, Janie. I just knew you'd be getting *it* real soon." Then she noticed you, diary! "Oh, let me see. I *love* diaries!"

She started to grab you, but I pulled you back and stuck you in my notebook. I told her, "Not *my* diary, Maureen. It's *private*—that's the whole point of a diary."

"I suppose," Maureen halfheartedly agreed.

Don't worry, diary. No one will ever read these words but me!

Jane

P.S. I did go to gym, and ran as fast as ever.

April 10, 9:00 P.M.
Dear Diary,

Today's Saturday. Saturdays are sometimes pretty boring, but not today.

Around ten o'clock this morning Cathy appeared at our back door. She waved the newspaper at me. "Janie, I read your horoscope for today and came right over."

She was so excited that I thought she was going to tell me I was about to be in a terrible car accident or win the lottery.

"Listen," she said as she laid the paper out on the table and read. "'Gemini, this is your big day. You're developing in new directions. Take a significant step in your personal life and you will be rewarded twofold.'"

"What's it mean?" I asked.

"Don't you see," she answered, "today's the day for you to buy a bra. It's in the stars."

When Cathy says something's in the stars you don't argue with her, particularly when it means a shopping trip on what promises to be a boring day.

My mom agreed and gave me some money. Cathy and I headed for Abernathy's Department Store.

Even Cathy was a little embarrassed when we walked into the "Bra Boutique." Everywhere you looked—bras. Hundreds of bras in all colors and sizes.

We tried to appear casual as we browsed among the racks. Out of the corner of my eye I could see that the saleslady was heading our way. Cathy saw her too.

We grabbed two smallish pink numbers and ducked into the dressing room so we wouldn't have to talk to her. I wanted to pick out a bra, pay for it, and get out of there—fast.

Now, Cathy and I used to take bubble baths together when we were ten and think nothing of it. But I've got to tell you, dear diary, I felt embarrassed when I took my blouse off in front of her, particularly because she was staring right at my chest.

"One of your breasts is bigger than the other," she announced in a shocked, loud voice.

I gulped and took a look in the mirror. She was right! If you looked carefully you could see one was a little bigger than the other.

"What does it mean?" I asked her.

She was real concerned. "I don't know," she said sympathetically. "I hope you don't grow up lopsided." I told you she's a Libra and likes things to balance out.

I was even more concerned. I pictured myself trying to run in the Boston Marathon with lopsided breasts!

The dressing-room curtains suddenly whipped back and there, smiling at us, was the saleslady. "Did I hear someone mention the word 'breast'?"

There I was, half dressed in front of a complete stranger.

I hid behind Cathy while I buttoned my blouse closed. The saleslady wasn't embarrassed at all. "I'm Mrs. Bard. I couldn't help overhearing you. One of your breasts is bigger than the other. Am I right?"

I was speechless. All I could do was nod *yes*.

"Come on, girls, I have something to tell you." She pulled us out of the dressing room and sat us down on a little couch. "I've worked in this department for twenty-five years. I'm something of an expert on breasts."

She stood in front of us and launched into a lecture on *breasts*.

"Girls," she began, "your condition is absolutely normal. Breasts often grow at different rates. One a little slower. One a little faster. Some girls develop early. Some later on. Usually the two breasts end up matching one another in size. There's *nothing* to worry about. Next question."

That was a relief! By the time I'm ready to run in the marathon I should be evened out.

Cathy raised her hand like we were in school. She was really getting into this. "Can you figure out how big your breasts will be when you're all grown up?"

"Very good question, dear. What determines the size of your breasts is the genes you have inherited from your family. Since you can't be sure which traits you've inherited, most girls just have to wait and see."

Cathy leaned over and whispered, "I can't wait to tell Maureen about this."

The saleslady looked right at me. "Do you have a question, dear?"

I did. "Why," I asked her, "are big breasts supposed to be better?"

"My goodness!" She smiled as she shook her head. "Is there anything sillier in this world than all the fuss people make over the size of breasts? I say variety is the spice of life. With breasts, with people. Come with me and I'll show you what I mean."

She lead us back into the dressing rooms. This was getting to be a real adventure.

She threw open the curtain of the first dressing room. Cathy and I couldn't believe it. "Hello, Mrs. Stevens," she greeted a tall, big-busted woman in a black bra. "See girls, tall and full—wonderful."

Before Mrs. Stevens had a chance to say anything, we were on to the next dressing room.

She whipped the curtain open. A very surprised short, thin woman was tucking in her blouse.

"Notice," said our guide, "her breasts are much smaller than Mrs. Stevens, but equally wonderful, equally feminine."

There was one more dressing room to go.

"Excuse me, dear," the saleslady said as she opened the curtain on this short woman with medium-sized breasts. "I'm just showing these young ladies how lovely you are."

"Of course," said the woman, smiling at us. "You know, I used to wish my breasts were smaller, and my best friend wanted hers to be bigger. Now I'm glad I'm me, just the way I am."

"There," said the saleslady. "Lovely people, aren't they? Think how boring life would be if everybody looked the same. And all those magazine advertisements and TV shows make us think there is one perfect size we should all try to have. *Ri-dic-u-lous* is what I say. It's impossible. And besides, it would be very boring."

Mrs. Stevens came out from the dressing room ready to pay for her purchase. "Okay, girls," the saleslady said to us. "Go try something on. I'll be with you in a second."

As soon as she was out of earshot Cathy and I burst out laughing so hard we started to cry. We had a great time. I wish Maureen had come with us.

On the way home we talked about all the women we knew. As far as we could tell, none of them had the measurements that Maureen quoted as being the "perfect figure."

So, diary, I got a very little bra for my very little, uneven breasts. It's not pink, and it doesn't have any lace or ribbon, which I didn't want. But it's real soft and silky, which I did want.

Asking questions seems to be helping me with this growing-up business. I sure feel a lot better about myself.

But there are still some things I'm not sure about. Like, why do I feel all mushy down there sometimes? Maybe Mom will know how I can get some more information.

What a great day!

Jane

P.S. Maureen doesn't know I got a bra yet.

April 11
Dear Diary,

Well, diary, Mom came through with flying colors today. When I told her that I still had some questions about the changes I'm going through, she said, "I thought you might, and I know just where you can get the answers. Let's go to the bookstore *right now!*"

Ten minutes later we were in Bookmart looking around at thousands of books. "We'll ask the clerk for help," my mother announced. Just then two college students—guys—went to the register to pay for their books.

I detoured Mom into the mystery section.

As soon as the guys left she said, "Come on. There's nothing to be embarrassed about. I'll ask."

"I'd rather wait here," I told her.

I looked at the covers of the Agatha Christie books while Mom asked the clerk, "Do you have any books on puberty? For my daughter."

"Certainly," she said as she looked my way. "Why don't you both come with me?" I guess she saw us come in together.

Anyway, by then I wasn't so embarrassed.

The clerk showed us three books and I chose the one that looked like it was best for me.

My mom also bought a book called *Am I Normal?* for my "abnormal" ten-year-old brother. She says he must have questions about this kind of thing and that his body will start to change soon. I wish his personality would change.

My mom says he's perfectly normal for a ten-year-old boy and that my Uncle Louie was a miserable pest when he was *her* kid brother and that now he's practically her best friend. I'll believe it when I see it.

The book *I* got, dear diary, is terrific. I'm going to paste in six of the most important pages so I can go over them whenever I need to.

ABOUT PUBERTY

Between the ages of 9 and 16, girls go through the physical, emotional and sexual changes of puberty.

Their breasts start to develop, the hips widen, and the waist narrows. They grow taller.

Hair begins to grow—on the legs, under the arms, and in the pubic area.

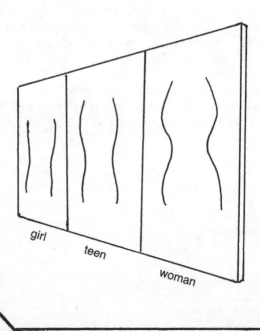

girl

teen

woman

During this time many girls may notice an occasional moistness in their underwear. This moisture comes out of the vagina and is called "vaginal discharge."

This may have a yellowish look, and will begin to happen about a year before a girl begins to menstruate—have her period. It's a perfectly normal part of growing up.

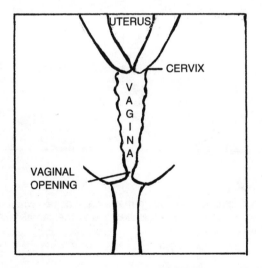

The vagina is a 3–4 inch passageway to the cervix, which is the opening into the uterus or womb.

Contrary to what a lot of people may think, the vagina is *not* an endless tunnel into your body—and nothing can "get lost" there!

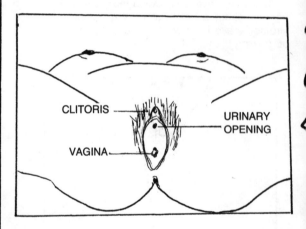

It is through the vagina that a baby comes when it is born. Also, vaginal discharge and menstrual flow come out of the vagina.

During puberty girls become aware of their sexual feelings.

You may know this is happening to you because you may suddenly feel nervous around boys...

Like that day on the track with Roger!

...or get a jumpy feeling in your stomach when you watch a romantic movie.

You may become aware of your body in a new way.

Often sexual feelings will result in a sensation of wetness in the vaginal area, and a feeling of dampness in the underwear.

So that's what

Maureen was talking about when

she was giving me that kissing lesson!

All of these changes are caused by hormones, which are chemicals produced by your body. They are released into your bloodstream and trigger the physical and emotional changes of puberty.

These changes can be surprising at times—but they're all PERFECTLY NORMAL!

The vagina and the clitoris are centers of sexual feeling in women. Many girls and women find it pleasurable to stimulate themselves by touching these parts of their bodies. This is called MASTURBATION. Sometimes they will do this until they experience an intense, pleasurable feeling called ORGASM.

Many people (men *and* women) masturbate, because it gives them pleasure or relaxes them. It is also a way of getting to know their bodies and feeling good about them. Other people do not enjoy it, or may find it against their principles.

Masturbation cannot hurt you if you do it, and it can't hurt you if you don't. It's totally up to you.

It's normal to do it and it's normal not to!

The last sentence in the book made me feel best of all: "It is natural to be concerned with all these changes your body is going through—but it's all perfectly normal."

Good night.

Jane

P.S. I feel much better about myself.
P.P.S. It's sort of fun to wear a bra.

3:00 P.M., April 12
Dear Diary,

I'm sitting on the bleachers thinking about what happened to me just now and have decided to write it all down. (I'm glad I brought you to school today!)

Remember how much better I was feeling about myself and how I said I had a handle on this puberty business and felt like I was finally catching up with my friends?

Well, Maureen and Cathy seem to be way ahead of me again.

This is what happened.

The three of us were sitting on the bleachers after school just talking and fooling around. They decided that while I ran they'd go check out who was in the Sub Shop. Just then a couple from the sophomore class passed us. The guy had his arm around the girl and they stopped every few steps to kiss and stuff.

Maureen got that moony-loony look she has when she talks about boys. "Going steady. I can't wait My life will be so-o-o perfect!"

"Yeah," Cathy sighed. "I just wish I could find the right guy."

I thought about going steady for a minute and told them, "I'm not in such a hurry to go steady. Maybe I'll wait until next year."

"Wait until next year!" they both shouted. You'd think I committed a crime or something.

"What's wrong with that?" I asked.

Maureen sighed. "Janie, I'll be honest with you. Not to want to go steady at your age, and with all the help we've given you on being a woman—well, it just isn't normal."

"Besides," Cathy added, "what if you got hit by a truck before next year or got lost in a desert or something else terrible happened so you never got to go steady? Your whole life—wasted!"

They went off to the Sub Shop and left me to do my run. But I don't feel like running anymore.

Is something wrong with me? It's true that Maureen and Cathy showed me how to kiss a boy and even tried to help me get a boyfriend.

I've gotten my period and I understand about why it happens and everything. I'm even wearing a bra now. But I don't want to go steady yet. I haven't even had a date with a boy. Maybe something *is* wrong with me.

I wish diaries could talk back.

Coach Anderson's putting the soccer equipment away. Now, she's the kind of woman I'd like to be when I'm finished with this growing-up business. She's nice and a great athlete...I wonder if she worried about going steady when she was in the seventh grade? She's a terrific running coach, maybe she could coach me on this. I'm going to try to talk to her.

Jane

P.S. I'll let you know what happens.

April 12
4:00 P.M.
Dear Diary,

I did it. I talked to Coach Anderson.

"Hi, Janie," she called when she saw me coming toward her. "I don't see you running today. What's up?"

"Ah, I was waiting for you, coach. I—I wanted to ask you something." I was suddenly tongue-tied.

Coach looked up and smiled. "You can talk to me about *anything*, Janie. You know that." It was almost like she read my mind. "Come here. Let's sit down for a while."

We sat down together on the edge of the field. I tried to swallow my nervousness and told her, "Well, I've been confused about the way I feel about myself lately."

She nodded. "Do I ever remember that feeling! What's been happening lately to make you feel confused?"

I was still nervous. I started making a little pile of mowed grass so I'd have an excuse for not looking at her. Then I took a deep breath and told her what was on my mind. "All my friends are talking about going steady and I get nervous just talking to a guy. I don't feel ready, you know what I mean? Maybe my friends are right. Maybe I'm not normal."

She smiled. "Janie," she said, "part of growing up means becoming a woman. While that's happening it's natural to start having sexual feelings and to get interested in sex. It's scary sometimes, but it's wonderful too."

I nodded my head.

She looked straight into my eyes. "But listen, Janie. You don't have to do anything you don't want to do until *you're* ready. You see, everybody grows at a different rate."

Now, this is where she made the most sense.

"It's like running," she said as she moved her index and middle fingers like a runner's legs. "You have to pace yourself and listen to your own heart. Sometimes you need to go slow and catch your breath." Her fingers ran slowly through the grass.

"And at other times you feel like you're ready to really move ahead." Her fingers moved more quickly and leapt over the mound of grass. "It's the same with growing up."

She leaned forward and smiled at me. "I know there are a lot of pressures in your life—boys, school, friends—a whole world of pressures. But you don't have to do anything that doesn't feel right to *you*.

"It's your race, Janie. Go at your own pace. And I promise you, that way you'll win."

Isn't that terrific?

It's your race.

Go at your own pace.

That's it. That's the key to getting through this growing-up business.

I'm going for a nice long run and think some more about what the coach said.

Yours,

Jane

April 12, 9:00 P.M.
Dear Diary,

What a day!

After I wrote about my talk with coach, I started running the quarter-mile track. When I was half-way around I decided to go over to the Sub Shop to find Maureen and Cathy. But I missed them, so I ran back to the field.

Cathy met me. She looked upset. "Janie," she yelled. "You left your diary!"

That's when I remembered that I left you on the bleachers with my other books.

Cathy pointed across the playing field. "I think some girls have got it!"

I followed her pointing finger. There, at the opposite end of the field, was the entire Slim-Trim Exercise Club and Maureen huddled around a book—MY DIARY!

I was stunned. I couldn't let them read another word.

I took off across that field.

All my secret thoughts and feelings, all the things I've shared with only you—being read by just about everyone! I would never, *ever* be able to show my face in school again.

I ran faster and faster—I knew when I was half-way across the field that this was my fastest time ever.

That's when I started to get angry. How dare they read *my diary!*

I turned around. Cathy—running her fastest—wasn't even a third of the way across the field and I was already standing in front of the Slim-Trim Club.

I put my hands on my hips and glared down at them. How could they? How could they do this? I cleared my throat loudly.

Karen saw me first. She stopped reading as she nudged Marilyn. Marilyn gave a little "Oh," which alerted Teri, who poked Maureen.

Everyone looked at me. I was ready to explode. I opened my mouth to give them a piece of my mind when Karen suddenly got up. She came over and handed me you, dear diary. Then she put her arm around me and said, "Thank you, Janie. I thought I was the only one who felt that way."

Then Marilyn jumped up and came over. "Oh, Janie, I'm so relieved to find out that you feel that way too."

I couldn't believe it! All of a sudden the whole class was around me and talking at once.

They were so excited. I just couldn't believe it.
They kept patting me on the back and jumping up
and down. It was like I won the Best in County at
the track meet.

I felt great!

Maureen came over to me. Even though every
thing was turning out all right, I didn't want to le
her get away with this. "Maureen," I said, "how
could you let them read my diary?"

She put her arm around me and smiled. "Bu
Janie, I knew it would make everyone feel bette
about all this teen-age stuff. You don't mind helpin
your friends out, do you? I mean, what are frienc
for, anyway?"

"Maureen," I said, "gimme a break. You were ju
dying to read my diary."

The three of us walked home together, like always. We were still talking about my diary and how much everybody liked it when we got to my house, so Cathy and Maureen came in.

Maureen sat on the bed hugging my smile pillow. She blushed a little. "I've got a confession to make. You know all that stuff you wrote in your diary. Well, I feel that way too sometimes."

Even the great Maureen! I was amazed and sort of relieved. "Don't worry, Maureen," I reassured her. "It's perfectly normal."

She threw the pillow at me. "By the way, Janie, I figured out how we can get Roger to notice you." She grabbed an issue of *Teen Scene* magazine from her notebook and flipped through it. "Listen, 'Thirteen Ways to Catch That Special Guy.' One of these has got to be the *perfect* way to catch Roger. Now pay attention. 'Number One.—'"

I threw my stuffed kangaroo at her. "Forget it, Maureen. I'm not catching anyone—not this week, anyway."

Maureen winked at me as she threw the kangaroo at Cathy. "Well, then, let's help *Cathy* lay a trap for Tommy Granger."

"Oh, no, you don't. Not *me.*" Cathy protested. She threw the kangaroo back at Maureen and a pillow at me.

Before you knew it we were having a terrific pillow fight—our best ever.

Diary, I love my friends. They're the greatest.

And now they know our secrets. I guess in a way it's all right, because now *I* know that other girls have the same feelings I have—even Maureen and Cathy. And I know for sure that we're all real normal.

But diary, do you see this double line?

From this line on, no one will read you or know
my secret thoughts.
I swear it.

Love,

Janie

P.S. I guess Janie is an all-right name—for now.
P.P.S. Maybe, instead of being a dentist when I
grow up, I'll be a writer.

JEANNE BETANCOURT has taught junior high and high school, designed and taught courses in film and television, and run film programming workshops for librarians and educators. She is a contributing editor of *Channels* magazine, and is on the board of advisors of the Media Center for Children. Her published work includes articles and reviews and non-fiction for young readers. She currently lives with her daughter and her husband in New York City, where she is at work on a novel called THE RAINBOW KID.

DEBRA FRANCO and DAVID SHEPARD are a filmmaking/writing team based in New York. Ms. Franco is vice president of New Day Films, a distribution cooperative of award-winning filmmakers. Mr. Shepard is a former film editor for public television and is the co-author of several screenplays. They are currently working on a feature film about adolescence.

AM I NORMAL? and DEAR DIARY are available as films for rental and purchase to schools and educational institutions from:

New Day Films
P.O. Box 315
Franklin Lakes, N.J. 07417

AM I NORMAL? and DEAR DIARY are also available on videocassette and disc for home use. For more information, please write to:

MGM/UA Home Video
1700 Broadway
New York, N.Y. 10019